Growing Stories

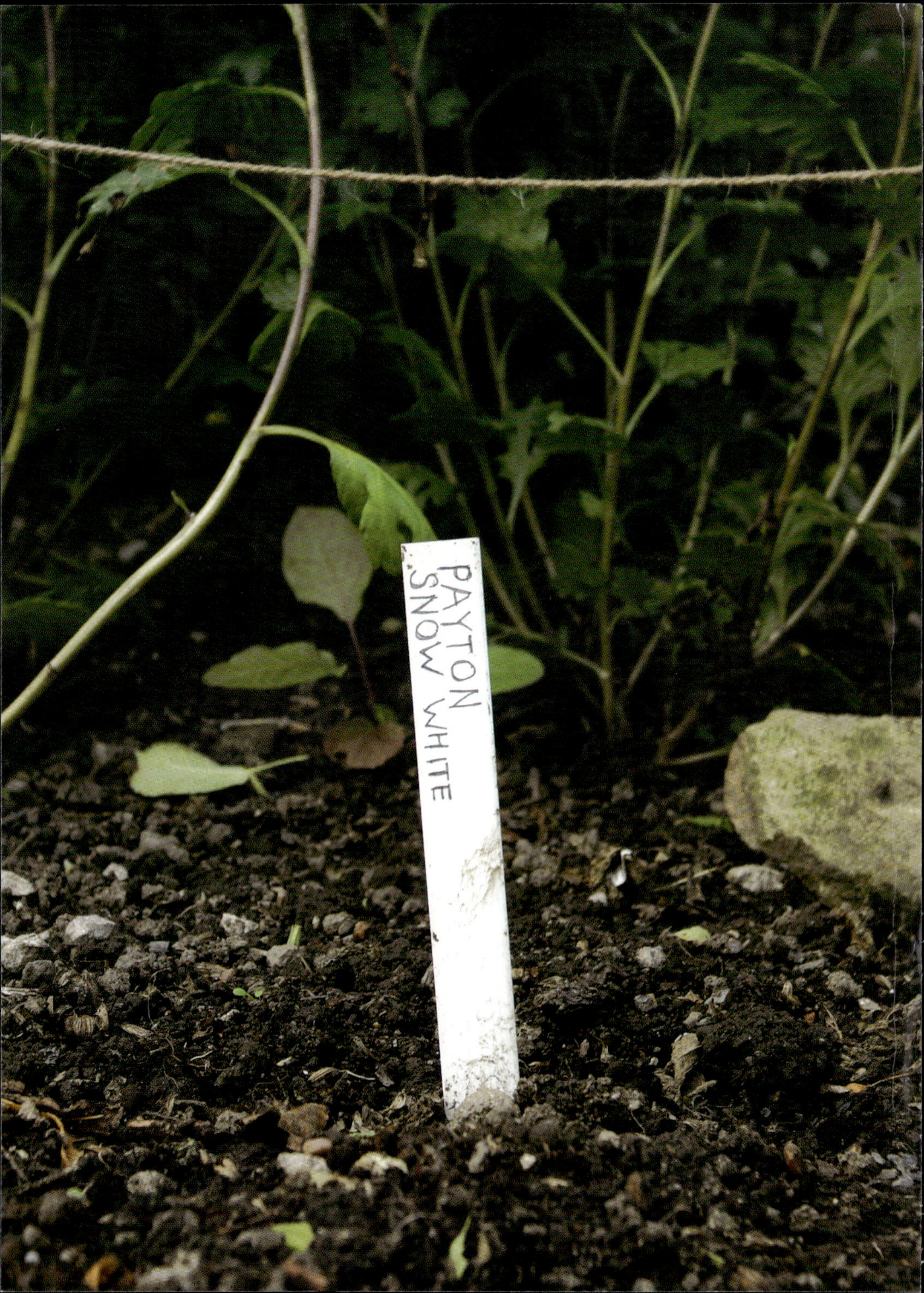
PAYTON
SNOW WHITE

Glassball Art Projects

Growing Stories

First published 2008
by Glassball Art Projects
www.glassball.org.uk

Designed and typeset by Gerhard Stromberg
Printed in the UK by The Cromwell Press,Trowbridge, Wiltshire.

ISBN 978-0-9558060-0-1

Supported by
The National Lottery®
through the Heritage Lottery Fund

Heritage
Lottery Fund

Glassball **Art Projects**

DERBYSHIRE
DALES

DISTRICT COUNCIL

CHATSWORTH

Frontispiece
Louise Wallwork, *Snow White*

Growing Stories

Contents

Foreword 7

Introduction and Acknowledgements 9

A Brief History of the Gardens at Chatsworth 13

The Working Garden 21

Oral History: Sean Doxey 31

The Pleasure Garden 37

Oral History: Jim Link 49

The Landscape Garden 55

List of Participants 64

Jake Cundy, *During The War*

Foreword

Chatsworth is a living place entangled with the concept of the Peak District and rooted in its earth. The house stands reflected in the waters of the River Derwent, shouldering the bleak East Moor from which its stone is quarried, an epicentre from which gardens, woods and parkland rush out to the horizon. Chatsworth exists at a frontier between culture and nature. It is a product of its landscape, which it has in turn transformed. It is endlessly changing and constantly renewed to meet the imaginings of every new generation.

Change is a tradition here, but it is enacted with one eye on the past, and treasures from past centuries are preserved. So the place is heavy with history, and history can be an overwhelming thing. But, there are as many stories of Chatsworth as there have been characters that have lived in, worked in, and visited the place – some are remembered, some are told, most have been forgotten. New stories are still to be made.

This book captures a moment in the stories of a group of young people who spent a summer exploring the garden at Chatsworth. Inspired by their past experiences of visiting the landscape, they returned determined to discover more and to form a creative group response. We have been very lucky to be able to take part in this project, and to share in the results. It is not unusual for young people to record their imaginative reactions to Chatsworth, but it is a rare opportunity to be able to see, keep and share these reactions. *Growing Stories* has grown out of Chatsworth and its characters, which it will, in turn, transform.

Claire Fowler
Education Officer
Devonshire Educational Trust

A house is bricks and mortar,
But a garden makes a home.

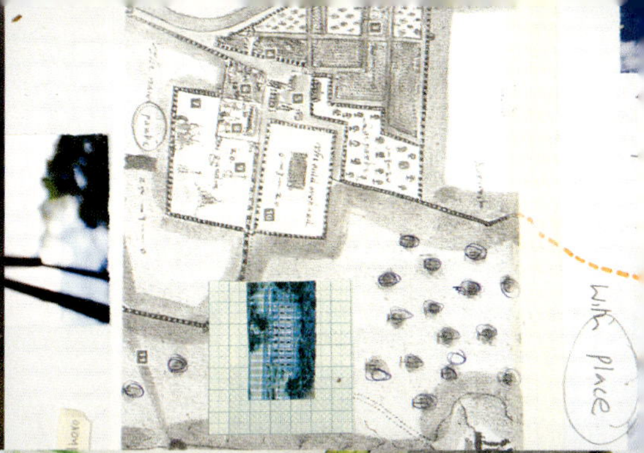

With Place?

Vegetable of Marlow Basil Sumner's Savory Kidney Pipstone

5 MILES OF FOOTPATH

THIC FOOTPA

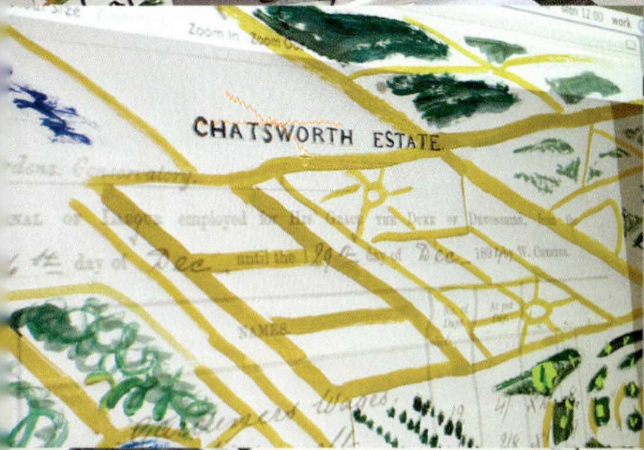

CHATSWORTH ESTATE

CHATSWORTH ESTATE
NAMES

employed for His Grace the Duke of Devonshire
day of Dec until the 19th of Dec

Sunday Duty

Josh Sheldon
Jessie Towndrow
John Young
William Sheldon
George Hulley
Elias Morton
George Askey
George Frith
James Stone
John Evans
1896 I certify that the above amounts are
correct and have been paid by me. Wm Chester

GRAND CONSERVATORY

Introduction and Acknowledgements

The idea for *Growing Stories* developed out of a previous project, *Fictitious Landscapes,* in which a group of young people explored the landscape, history, and culture of the Derbyshire Dales, using digital media. During our research for *Fictitious Landscapes* the group also visited Chatsworth, where we were shown around the house and gardens. Although none of the art works produced for *Fictitious Landscapes* referred to Chatsworth, the group chose its wonderful Victorian theatre as the venue for the local launch of the three short films and the book, which became the results of that project.

Maybe unexpectedly, it soon evolved that our initial visit and the great atmosphere of our evening in Chatsworth's theatre had made lasting impressions on the group, and had stimulated their curiosity. During our feedback sessions, nearly all of them expressed the wish to explore the history and significance of Chatsworth further, and urged us to develop a project that would focus on its gardens. We held a consultation workshop to advance this idea and to interest new participants. Once a new group was established, we engaged the young people in all aspects of setting up the proposed project, from funding applications to issues of scheduling and transport.

Thankfully we could secure the necessary funding and support, and at the start of the summer holiday in 2007 a group of twelve 14–17-year-olds began the work on *Growing Stories*. Generously, the Devonshire Educational Trust granted us not only access to extensive areas of the house and gardens and their staff, but also the use of a spacious hall within the estate's office complex for our meetings.

An important part of the project work consisted of research into the history of the gardens at Chatsworth. Here, we could draw on the estate's own extensive archives and collections, as well as on conversations with present and past employees. The rare opportunity to engage with the meticulously documented history of Chatsworth, no doubt greatly informed each participant's creative process. We had the chance to see, for example, letters to Sir Joseph Paxton and journals from plant expeditions. We could study the collection of historic photographs, from rare 19th century prints to early colour photographs from the 1950s, and make our own very real journey through photography's history. But, we also had access to down-to-earth ledgers, recording centuries of diligent housekeeping. To further help the participants in the development of their own creative approaches, we also invited several consultants to advice the group, from an oral history specialist, through artists working with film and photography, to the book's designer.

This book and its enclosed DVD hope to celebrate the work of the young people who took part in *Growing Stories*. The work you can see here represents, one could say, 'the tip of the iceberg,' the bit that prettily glistens in the Arctic light between sea and sky. I am confident that you too will enjoy this showcase of photographs, texts and films for their beauty, their intelligence, and their real engagement with the subject matter. The role of Chatsworth as a major tourist attraction and its imposing presence might suggest that it could be hard for young people from the area to connect with it. *Growing Stories,* no doubt, proves this notion wrong.

As an organisation working with art development and education for young people, the "hidden parts of the iceberg" are of central importance to Glassball Art Projects. It is, of course, momentous to see a young person, say, begin to use his or her mobile phone as a creative tool; but of equal importance is the recognition that the creative process, with its demands on all aspects of a personality, can enrich and empower young people far beyond the tangible results of their efforts.

This book and DVD would not have been possible without the enthusiasm and commitment of the young people involved. We and the participants would like to thank Tina Ball (REAP Project Director), Ruth Gordon (Local Studies Development Librarian), Colin Hyde (East Midlands Oral History Archive) and Amanda Turner (Heritage Lottery Grant Officer) for their help and guidance. Our special thanks go to Adrian Brocklebank, Sean Doxey, Marcus Goodwin, Stefan Homerski, Jim Link, Diane Naylor, John Oliver, Steve Porter, David Spencer, Mick Thraves and Ian Webster for allowing us to record their memories and thoughts. Thank you also to David Ball and Kate Luxford, the artists involved and to Andrew Pepitt and Stuart Band, Chatsworth Archivists. We are also grateful to the Duke and Duchess of Devonshire for hosting this project, and their permission to reproduce materials from their archive and collection. Finally, we would like to thank Dawn Goodfellow, Shenagh Firth and Claire Fowler from the Devonshire Educational Trust for their support and priceless advice.

Cora Glasser
Project Co-ordinator, Glassball Art Projects

A Brief History of the Gardens at Chatsworth

Half the interest of a garden is the constant exercise of the imagination.
Mrs. C. W. Earle, *Pot-Pourri from a Surrey Garden,* 1897

Every Duke of Devonshire, from Stuart times to the modern day, has attempted to leave a lasting mark on the grounds of Chatsworth. The gardens as we see them today, with contemporary additions to an informal, but still tightly planned 19th century design, carry features from every period of Chatsworth's development. The Renaissance formal gardens have long disappeared, but elements remain in the form of a rose garden with four square beds and central walkways. Next to it are the 18th century Salisbury lawns, side-by-side and nestling nicely together. I remember sitting on these lawns as a child during visits with my family.

One of my favourite features of the gardens is the imposing Cascade, built during the tenure of the 1st Duke and finished in 1696. In 1702 it was extended and the Cascade House was added. During the 1830s the 6th Duke had the Cascade, and its house, moved to be in line with a newly formed gravel path up the slope. I have memories of being a small child on family days out, paddling in the Cascade and having much fun in its running water. Today, it is the different sounds of the water, as it runs down over the 24 steps, that fascinate me. This sound changes as the water runs over stone slabs of varying length, width and height, and creates an ever-changing tune as you walk up or down along it.

Although there remain many more details from the earliest designs, the gardens, as they present themselves today, are mainly from the period of the 6th Duke, William Spencer Cavendish (1790–1858). He met a young gardener, Joseph Paxton, who was then working in gardens near one of the Duke's London homes, Chiswick House. The Duke found his work so intriguing that he appointed Paxton, who was then only 23 years old, as the head gardener of Chatsworth.

Paxton set about planning a great shake-up of the garden to bring it up to date. His plans still survive today in the form of a massive scroll, detailing everything that was to happen. Paxton and the 6th Duke integrated some of the older features of the garden, and complemented them with newer trends and technological advances.

Joseph Paxton also sent out expeditions to discover new species of plants and trees in exotic places, which he then had sent back to Chatsworth and kept in newly designed and built 'hothouses'. These were vast glass conservatories with a complex system of flues and hot water pipes to keep the temperatures up to tropical levels!

The greatest of these structures was aptly named the Great Conservatory. This enormous structure was designed by Paxton and is seen as the forerunner to his famous Crystal Palace, which housed the Great Exhibition of 1851. Building began in 1836, and the conservatory was finished and planted in 1840. At the time it was the largest conservatory in the world, but unfortunately it is not here today. During the Great War, because of a lack of personnel to maintain it and coal to keep its tropical temperature, it became impossible to retain it, and in 1920 the decision

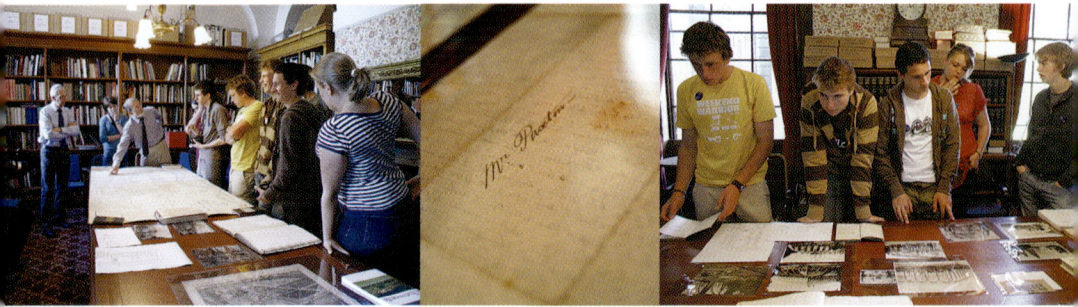

was made to demolish it. Paxton's structure, however, was to prove its strength by withstanding two attempts to blow it up and only surrendering on the third attempt. Glass from it flew everywhere, and shards of this glass can still be found to this day, if you are lucky! My favourite story of this demolition is about the house itself, where a shard came in through a library window and was embedded firmly into a book. If only the Great Conservatory had been kept! It would still be one of Chatsworth's most grand and awe-inspiring features.

The Great Conservatory was not the only 'hothouse' that Paxton had built. He designed many more, and the one I like most is the Conservative Wall, or the Case. This structure runs the span of the northern wall of the gardens where the current entrance is located. It was completed by 1842, two years after the Great Conservatory. It too was designed to retain heat and cultivate exotic plants at Chatsworth. I particularly like its architecture and form. It spans an uphill slope and follows this in segments that are linked by internal steps.

Paxton liked to do things on a grand scale, and he showed this desire again when he built the Rock Garden. Rock gardens were becoming fashionable in the 1840s, so the 6th Duke decided he was not one to be unfashionable and commissioned Paxton to build a rock garden on a massive scale. This Paxton did to amazing effect, with boulders the size of small cars. To move them in place, he invented a steam–powered lifting device. The rocks were placed to replicate some of the best-looking rock outcrops in the world, and this involved some rocks looking as though they could fall at any minute. The Rock Garden took six years to complete and, when it was finally inaugurated, he named three stacks after the Duke of Wellington, Prince Albert and Queen Victoria.

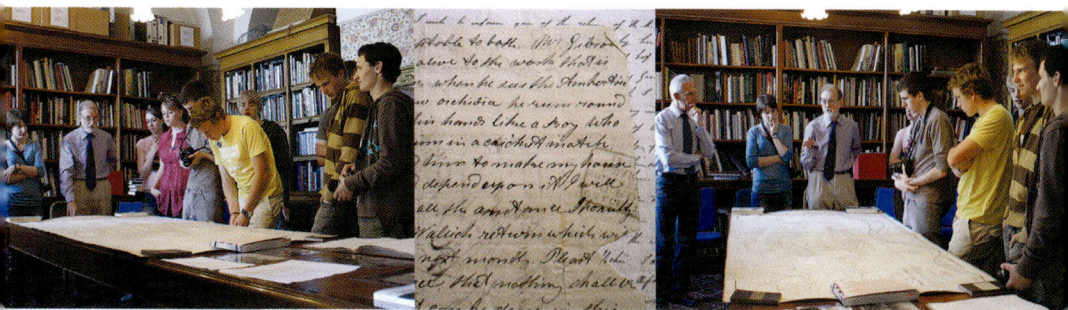

The group in the study room at Chatsworth

Today the Rock Garden still looks as impressive as it did then. The rocks are big and imposing, and really make you feel small. Far from intimidating me, they made me think about their natural beauty, which is often overlooked. As you pass underneath them, the rocks frame your view, giving a natural frame to a man-made scene. The plants complement this natural look and seem to have colonised this area of their own accord instead of following a meticulous design.

Paxton also replaced the 1st Duke's Great Fountain with the Emperor Fountain, named after Czar Nicholas I. The Czar was expected to be visiting Chatsworth in 1844 and the Duke thought it would be good if the Czar could see a fountain higher than his own at the Imperial Palace in St Petersburg. Paxton had the Emperor Fountain built, but the Czar never came to see it. The fountain, though, broke the height record for a gravity fed fountain by reaching 296 feet.

A single 16-inch wide pipe carries water from the lakes above Chatsworth, which also feed the other fountains, to the Emperor Fountain. The fountain then fires the water up into the air. On a still day the fountain can reach massive heights and can be seen above the tree tops from down the valley, and from most places in the park. I am always struck by how high the fountain can actually reach and stunned that this height is achieved only using gravity. It is one of those majestic things that can seem so tranquil, although much force is used to get it to those heights.

Probably the least visited sections of the park are more of Paxton's creations, the Pinetum and Arboretum. Paxton and the 6th Duke created these collections, finding some of the most beautiful specimens from throughout the world. The Pinetum and Arboretum are at the southern edge of the park, and their paths are not as well trodden as those around the Rock Garden. I like the size of

the trees and the tranquillity of the atmosphere because people are few and far between. It is one of those places I can lose myself in for hours, looking at the different specimens in each collection.

Although much of the garden, as we experience it today, stems from Paxton's era, it has not stopped evolving and continues to evolve today. My favourite contemporary part of the garden is one that still serves the family today. The Kitchen Garden, in its current position, was planted in 1994 and supplies the current Duke and his family with fruit and vegetables. Although other sections of the park were used in the past for this purpose, a full Kitchen Garden was only resurrected after the garden at Barbrook, half a mile away in the park, was closed down in 1946. The smells of the wide variety of herbs growing there really gets to me as I walk around it, and it is also a comfort to see that, although the larger parts of the gardens are used for pleasure, the gardens are still worked to supply produce for the house.

Although the main garden is probably the best-known part of Chatsworth's grounds, my personal favourite, and where I hold most of my memories about Chatsworth, is the surrounding park, which was designed by Capability Brown (1716–1783) in the early 18th century. It is here that I have gone on many walks with family and friends, had picnics with my parents, gone to the Peak 2000 Scout Camp, and it is the place where I now work in the garden centre. The scenery is just so beautiful, and you are forever finding new delights, like the Swiss Cottage up near the lakes. Walking in the park always brings hours of fun and precious time with family and grandparents. I would say I am lucky to have been brought up living

Photographs from the Devonshire Collection

so close to the park, and I would like to carry on using its facilities, and maybe one day I will bring my own grandchildren.

I feel what Chatsworth does really well is to connect the old with the new. This happens not only in the house and the gardens, but also socially, between the young and the old. I have heard many stories about Chatsworth from other people's youth, and I will, I am sure, be passing mine on too. Gardens are here to be enjoyed by every generation, and the gardens at Chatsworth House are a prime example of this pleasure.

Jake Cundy
Project Participant

Sir Joseph Paxton

Head Gardener	1826–1858
Richard George	1859–1861
William Thompson	1861–1863
William Laytham	1863–1864
George Scrimshaw	1865–1880
Thomas Speed	1880–1883
O. Thomas	1884–1891
W. Chester	1891–1906
Frank Jennings	1906–1920
G. F. Marples	1920–1924
J. G. Weston	1924–1940
Bert Link	1940–1974
Dennis Hopkins	1974–1989
Jim Link	1989–1999
Ian Webster	1999– present

Cora Glasser, *Edensor Village and Paxton's Grave*

The Working Garden

Joe Griffiths, *Tail Feathers*

pp 22/23
Louise Wallwork, *Kitchen Garden Glasshouses*

Joe Eatherden, *Keep In, Keep Out*

Louise Wallwork, *Found Plant Labels*

p 26
Jake Cundy, *Inside the Orchid House*
p 27
Jake Cundy, *Inside the Main Glass House*

Louise Wallwork and Kate Luxford, *Kitchen Garden*

Oral History: Sean Doxey

Father was from Derbyshire, born and bred. My father's side of the family worked as quarrymen. My mother was from Dublin, and came across in the 1940s. I was born in Wirksworth and have been in and around this area ever since.

I left school in 1977. It was quite a lucky time to leave school as everyone who left with me went into a job. Most of my friends went straight into apprenticeships, either at British Rail or with local tradesmen. I wasn't too sure what I wanted to do, but I was keen to work in the construction industry, making things. I was offered several positions in the area; one of them was as an apprentice joiner here at the house. If I had gone for the other jobs, in Derby or Wirksworth, I could of got to them by bus. But, I was desperate for a moped, this is true, and my parents said I was definitely not to have a moped. The only way I could get from where I lived to Chatsworth was on a moped, so I told my parents I wanted to work at Chatsworth. That's the only reason I came to work on this estate. It was, because I wanted a moped! And I've been here ever since, and it's been one of the best decisions I have ever made. I finished school on the Friday, started work at Chatsworth on the Monday, at the sweet age of 16, and I've been here ever since!

This is my 30th year here. I started as an apprentice joiner, then as the head house carpenter, and then the comptroller. Not controller but comptroller! Many years ago, you had travelling groups of people building stately homes. They would have foremen, clerks of works, architects, and a competent person in charge of the purse, the comptroller. This is how the title was retained, because, technically, this person was also in charge of the family's finances. In a modern organisation, what I do is more easily described as an 'operation manager'. I head the maintenance team, part of what we call the 'welcome team', which is car parking. I also run the events, such as the country fair or the horse trials, and finally I'm making sure the estate is ready for the general public, when they arrive first thing in the morning. Hopefully, the first thing you see when you arrive over that bridge is what we've got ready for you. I basically look after the outside of the house.

My first memory of Chatsworth is of clocks, the ticking clocks! I was very lucky when I started working at Chatsworth; it was almost like a time capsule. When I started it was nothing like the scale it is now. It's a unique place, this estate, in that you have villages on the estate. Everybody knows everybody else;

everybody lives in each other's pockets! After starting work here, people either loved it or hated it, and I loved it.

My first impression of the place was that I could not believe its size. I can remember walking into the private dinning room, which is where the family have their dinner, and the room was bigger than the house I grew up in. I walked into this room and thought "my God!" And I was blown away. The impression that will stay with me is that, wherever you go, you can hear a clock ticking; every room has a clock. There is one guy who goes round every Wednesday and winds up all the clocks, and wherever you are working, you can hear their ticking. When I was younger I used to think, "my God! I can hear my life ticking away in this place!" But it's an amazing place to be involved in.

The very first job I had to do here was to go and work on a set of stairs for a gypsy caravan. I got told off by my boss for doing such a poor job that I had to do them again. But, this caravan was in the chauffeur's garage. Inside this garage there was also the Bentley and a Morgan; the most incredible cars you could think of. And in this garage there were also all of the family's knick-knacks, the kids' bikes, go-carts, toys; it was just incredible!

So, after being here for about a month, I didn't really know what was in store for me in the future with regard to what my job would be here at the house, other than that it was made clear to me, when you start at Chatsworth, that the family comes first. And this is a philosophy that we've kept going, and also that job-wise you can be asked to do anything.

I've lived on the estate for about 22 years. I've lived in about four different houses on the estate. I now live up at Pilsley, in a fantastic house, very lucky, with wonderful views.

Other perks of the job are meeting lovely people, and as I live so close my commute to work is only four minutes. I don't have to sit in traffic. If you do get held up, it's usually a sheep or a pheasant on the road. There isn't one single aspect you like about working here, it's just an incredible place; it's the whole package.

I do get a variety of jobs to do, and most of these jobs are challenging. At this moment in time, I have just been trying to sort out Damien Hirst's sculpture. His studio has given permission to show it as part of the Sotheby's exhibition, and that has caused problems, as its 40 ft high, weights 14 tonnes and couldn't be installed where they originally wanted it.

There isn't anything I don't like about my job, but there are times, for example, when you're up on the moor trying to get streams unblocked, the rain's running down the back of your neck, and you think "oh my God!" But there really isn't anything I don't like; it's a great place to be involved with.

There is lot that changes here, visually through the seasons, obviously. We have a yearly programme of work and events, but work routines rarely change from year to year. We have a lot of maintenance work to do, some people refer to it as the 'Fourth Bridge' – once you come to the end you have to start all over again. I like seeing all of the seasons here at Chatsworth; every season brings its own key features to the place. This place looks fantastic the whole year round. I love walking up by the lakes. There is a little bit of this walk which takes you along by a very small crag. It's one of my favourite walks. I think that's a nice place to lose yourself if you can do that once in a while. My favourite area within the gardens is right at the back by the grotto pond, with a lovely little summer house set beside it. It's a very quite part of the gardens, because not a lot of people tend to walk out that far, which is a real shame.

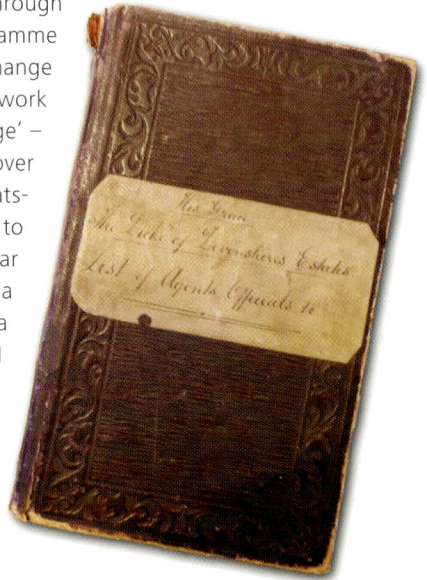

Stories? Well, there is a story about the gardeners. Many years ago all the estates used to brew their own beer, and we've got what they call the beer cellar here, and in there are big barrels that are empty now but they used to be full of beer. The brew house used to be in the stables, which is at the top of the hill, where the ladies toilets are now, that's where they used to brew the beer. So they used to brew this beer, and it was piped, through the gardens, to the cellar. Anyway, unbeknown to the powers that be, the gardeners had found where this pipe was, dug it up, exposed it and drilled a little hole in it and put a wooden bung in it. And every time a shipment of beer came down from the stables to the house, the gardeners had their own little private supply of beer!

Anybody working here on the estate, with the family living in the house, you walk past them or bump into them whilst they are here. They don't keep themselves to themselves. The previous Duke and Duchess used to walk about and made sure everyone was OK and it's the same now. I deal with them more on a professional basis. They come to me when they want jobs sorted, and things done. So I do have quite a bit of contact with the family.

Hopes for the future? I hope that Chatsworth remains the wonderful, magical place that it is. We have just come second in a consumer poll with regard to best visitor attraction, with Hampton Court coming first. I hope it stays as one of the top historical attractions in the country. That would be lovely.

Sean Doxey was born in 1961, and is the comptroller at Chatsworth. He was interviewed for Growing Stories *by Lorena Bramall.*

Daniel Fern, *Campbell's 1858 Plan of the Chatsworth Grounds*

The Pleasure Garden

Hannah Wallwork, *View of Blanche's Vase*

Lorena Bramall, *Secret Bridge*

pp 38/39
Jake Mycock, *At the Top of the Cascade*

Joe Eatherden, *A Hidden Window*

Jake Cundy, *The Cottage Garden*

Jake Cundy, *Flowers for the House*

Claire Wallwork, *The Conservative Wall*

Ruby Westnedge, *The Temple*

Ruby Westnedge, *Lily Pond*

Claire Wallwork, *Found Statues*

Oral History: Jim Link

My father came to this area from Kent when he was 19 years old, and my mother was born in Beeley, which is the village just down the road from Chatsworth. It was great to grow up around here. If you remember, in those days there was no television and just the wireless to listen to, so we were always out playing cricket or football. Around springtime we used to collect young jackdaws and have them as pets, and if we were cycling back from school at Baslow, they would be waiting for you in the trees. As soon as they got old enough, they would fly off with the other Jackdaws. They were great times.

My father was a gardener and finished up being the head gardener at Chatsworth, and he worked there for 50 years. My mother did domestic work and also helped out in the gardens, in the pay boxes that they had in those days.

I was six years old when the war started so that was quite a frightening thing, that's got to stick in your mind. I can remember my father didn't get called up. He stopped behind to grow the vegetables and other horticultural things to keep everybody going. We were lucky really, we didn't see much of the war, apart from seeing the army use Chatsworth as a training ground. I don't know if anyone has told you, but there is a bullet still lodged in a table in the house, where the Americans machine-gunned us! We were kids playing on the lawns and the bullets where coming through and smashing the windows and into the trees. Then there were two German planes that came down the valley; I can remember them. You can still see the shell marks on Chatsworth House at the front. We were waving at them at the time, we thought they were ours, you know, until they opened fire. Some other planes dropped incendiary bombs on Beeley Moor, and they thought they had hit something big, you know.

When I was at school I wanted to be anything from a lorry driver to a bus driver, oh anything. I didn't go into gardening, I went into forestry. At 15 years, you think using axes and saws and cutting big trees down, that's something exciting.

My first job was good, working with a big gang of men. They were good times. You worked with some young and some at the older end. You got your leg pulled and everything, but it was good planting trees. I can look back now at woods; some have been cut down now, that we planted. It wasn't great money,

Joe Eatherden, *Glasshouse*

agricultural wages, so we were on piecework. It was on how many trees you planted or cut down, or how many acres of bracken you cleaned round the young plants. It was hard work, but they were good times. I was never clever enough to go to university so you just went where work was local. People didn't travel great distances in those days. I've lived on the estate, in the same house, for nearly 50 years. It's been amazing living here, it's my home and I've brought up a family here.

As I said, my first job here was in the forestry, and you did anything from lorry driving to delivering to the pits, pit props in those days. I was in charge of a nursery, where they were growing young trees. I had a gang of about eight to ten men. They formed a new department, the domain department, which was responsible for the villages, the roads, trees, hedges, drains, and anything anyone else didn't want. I used this gang of men to start up this new department. I loved that, I was at home doing that kind of work. Then the head gardener wasn't very well, Dennis Hopkins, who I have great respect for. They asked me if I could help out, which I did. Then they said would I be the assistant to Dennis Hopkins and help on the outside, and I did this as well as look after the domain. Then that went on, and when Dennis retired they asked me if I wanted to be head gardener. So I had quite a build up, going up to this position. Lucky man really. I had no idea that I would be head gardener when I first started; it never entered my head.

I really enjoyed working here, for one you had two really good people to work for and I was doing things I liked. If you ever look at Stand Wood, the house has got to have a backdrop to it and we had to take out all the rhododendrons, and do the replanting, as no young trees were able to grow there, and it was the same in the gardens. This gives me pleasure, when I walk round today and see what I was part of. It wasn't my doing; it was what Her Grace at the time wanted. Her

Grace would ring in the morning, 7:55 am and say what she wanted and it was good; I was creating things. There are things in the gardens that I can look at, don't get me wrong, it's not me who did it. Well I cleared up after Paxton because he made a mess; sorry, I'm joking. There's no disputing what a great man he was, and his work is there to be seen. And somebody like Paxton must have had good men underneath him. I was lucky I had good staff and it's so important to have people who you respect, and they respect you.

My favourite place is the Pinetum. You can see the old trees planted in the old park. I go with my dogs at night, and it's just so peaceful up there. It helps you to think about what you have got to do the next day. The least favourite part of my job was all that form filling you had to do. I wasn't brought up to do that! Oh well, never mind.

Spring was my favourite season. When everything starts anew and fresh again. Work changed over the seasons, but in the winter you did your big jobs, say if a tree had got fungus and had to come down, you did that then. You prepare for spring, when things have to be sown and planted ready for next year. All the daffodil bulbs go in, and then it goes on. Well, you've just got to see those lawns, grass cutting starts and you've got to do the hedges. I used to know how many miles of hedges we had to cut, but I can't remember now; it was a lot.

My favourite changes since I've been here is the replanting of trees, and we set up the Kitchen Garden. There haven't been any great big changes really. Well, the introduction of machinery, that's been a development for the estate. There wasn't that much of a difference in work when my father was there and when I was working there, apart from the machinery. They still had to cut the hedges. We had far better machinery than what my father had. And the machinery again has improved in the last eight years, since I retired. It was all done by hand at one time. In my dad's days, it was all horse and cart. You imagine him coming back now and seeing all these tractors. Everyone walked everywhere then. The biggest change that happened in my life is machinery. It's still a good job, and I wish I could go on working. All I want now is my health and to just keep going on and enjoying my life.

We had laughs. I can remember in the forestry we had a foreman, a grand bloke, and we were plant cleaning in Beeley. That's where you clear with a sickle, when trees are about two to three foot tall, you cut the undergrowth from around them. So, there would be eight of you, and these trees were planted in rows, and you would cut the bracken or whatever away from the trees. This particular morning we were walking up to this plantation, taking our time, and the foreman came on his bike and started shouting that the boss was coming. So we all ran down to the bottom of the bank, and when we got there in a panic, we had all forgotten our sickles, we'd left them on the top. So we are there with our hands going through the motions, with nothing in them. The forester came along and said, "you've got a lot of spare sickles here, I'll take these back." So, he took a load and there we were, in the middle of nowhere with no sickles, no tools to use. This foreman went hairless; I can see him now!

I'm a bit of a beggar for setting people up sometimes, and we'd got this young girl coming along to start work on patrol. They have a garden patrol, and it was April Fool day. I told them, this is when the zoo was going, that two wolverines had escaped, and they've been reported this way. I gave them these sticks and told them not to tell the public, as there might be panic. "If you do see anything call the switchboard." So, after a while she cottoned on and vowed to get me back. Well after a long while, she must have been planning her revenge; she got me good and proper. I used to have this suit that I would wear if I was doing any spraying. Well, I needed help to get into this suit to go and do some spraying up at the Pinetum. She was ever so helpful; I should have guessed something was up. Anyway, I was making my way to the Pinetum, when I walked past the greenhouse and the lads started to laugh. I told them to get on with their jobs and carried on walking up to the bottom of the cascade. There were lots of families there at the time, and they all started laughing. It was then that I realised that she had sewn onto my suit two long ears and a fluffy tail! So, there was I, the head gardener, walking through the gardens looking like a rabbit. I suppose I had that one coming, she got me back! Yeah, we had some good laughs.

Jim Link, born in 1934, started working at Chatsworth in 1950, and was the head gardener between 1989 and 1999. He was interviewed for the project by Jake Mycock.

Louise Wallwork, *The Hundred Steps*

The Landscape Garden

Daniel Fern, *A Walk in the Grounds*

Chris Thornton, *View through Tree*

pp 56/57
David Ball, *The Grotto Pond*

Joe Eatherden, *Hard Edge*

Hannah Wallwork, *Path by the Grotto Pond*

Jake Cundy, *Looking into the Past*

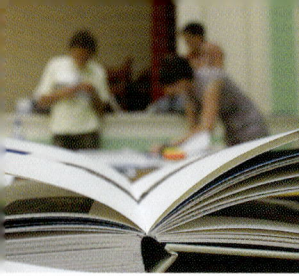

Growing Stories

Participants

Lorena Bramall, 17, Calver

Jake Cundy, 16, Darley Dale

Joe Eatherden, 16, Matlock

Daniel Fern, 17, Matlock

Tom Geddes, 16, Winster

Joe Griffiths, 17, Matlock

Jake Mycock, 17, Over Haddon

Chris Thornton, 17, Bakewell

Claire Wallwork, 17, Darley Dale

Hannah Wallwork, 13, Matlock

Louise Wallwork, 14, Darley Dale

Ruby Westnedge, 15, Holloway

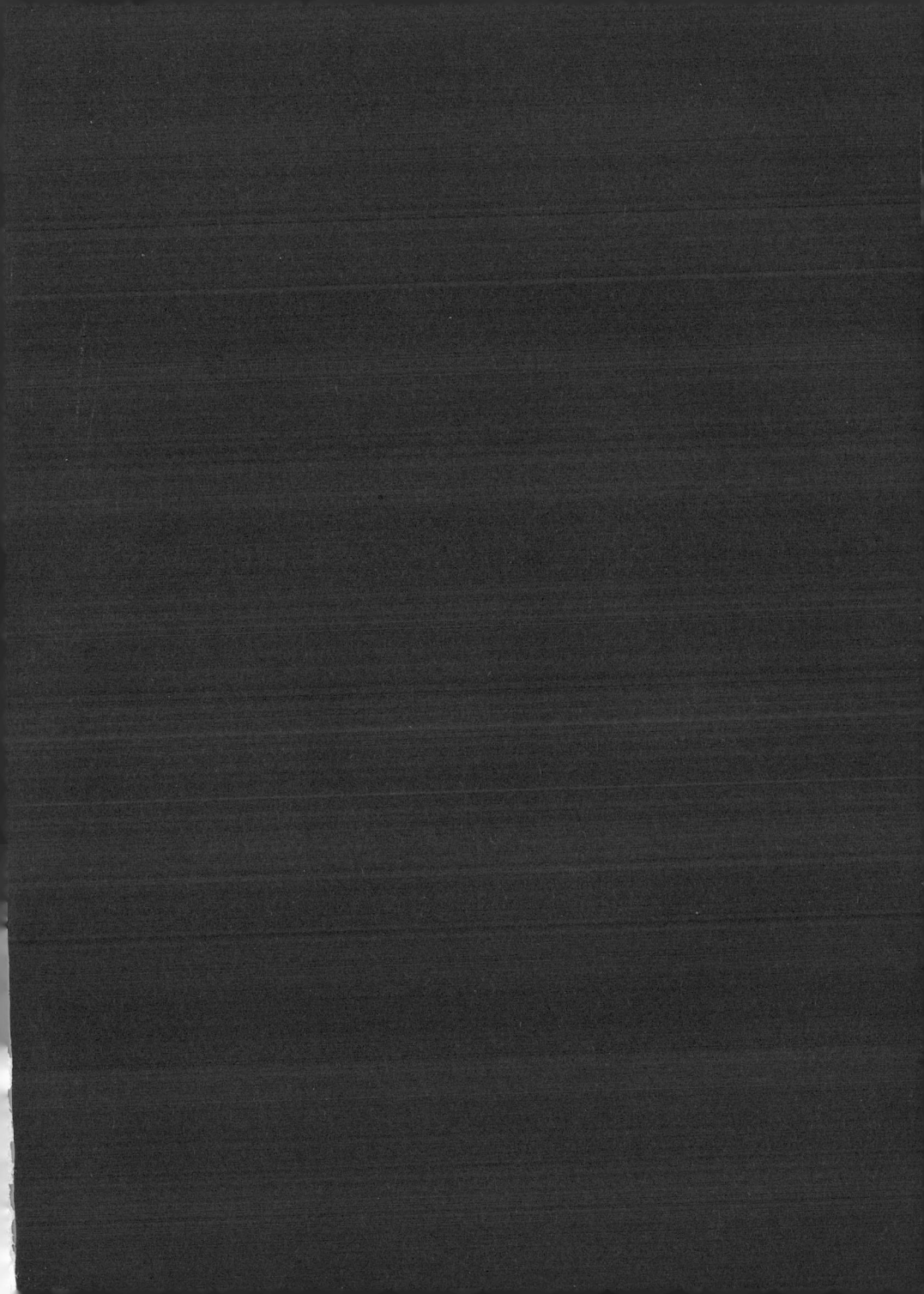